I0122095

FREEDOM 2 CHANGE™

The Experience
Workbook One

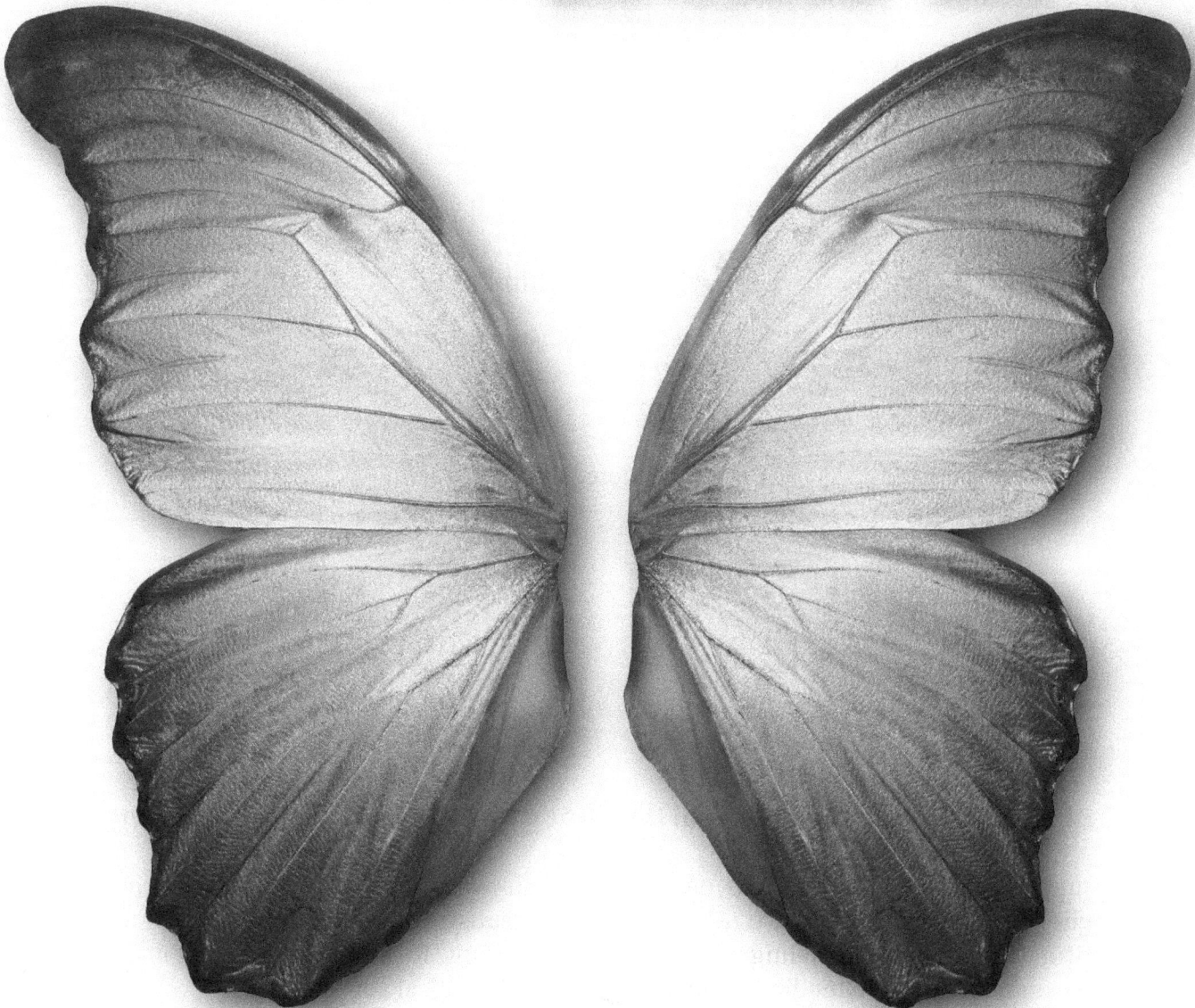

Gregory L. Little, Ed.D.

Kimberly J. Prachniak, M.S.

& Stanley W. Prachniak, M.B.A.

Freedom2Change Workbook 1: The Experience

Copyright © 2019 by Gregory L. Little, Kimberly J. Prachniak, & Stanley W. Prachniak

All rights reserved.

No part of this book may be reproduced or utilized in any form or by any means, electronic or mechanical, including photocopying, recording, or by any other information storage and retrieval system, without permission in writing from the publisher.

All photos and illustrations in this book are licensed.

ISBN 10: 0-9655392-3-7
ISBN 13: 978-0-9655392-3-4

⟲FREEDOM2CHANGE™

Freedom2Change.org
PO Box 9025
Memphis, TN 38190

www.freedom2change.org

DISCLAIMER—Seek Professional Help If You Need Therapy Or Medical Advice

The methods, concepts, and ideas described in this workbook are the authors' personal thoughts and opinions. They are not intended as a substitute for medical advice, nor as a substitute for needed counseling or psychological therapy. Readers should consult licensed professionals for needed medical, counseling, or psychological services.

INTRODUCTION

There is three errers in this sentence.
Find them.

(The answer, if you don't get it, is found on page 18.)

This workbook, *The Experience,* is designed to follow the concepts and techniques out-lined in the book *Freedom To Change.* The subtitle of that book, *"Why You Are the Way You Are and What You Can Do About It,"* is the focus of this workbook. As we stated repeatedly in the main book, you have the ability to change just about anything in your life. But it is wise to carefully consider the changes you want to make before you make them. There is an old adage, "Be careful what you wish for, because you just might get it!" What we suggest here is that you think about the things you believe will lead you to happiness, and then challenge your beliefs about them. If you feel as if you are on the wrong path in life, it doesn't make much sense to go from one wrong path to another. So our recommendation is to seek out your True Path in life, then make decisions and act in accordance with your True Path. In *Freedom To Change,* the ideas of a True Path and a True or Higher Self are discussed several times. If you have a sense of satisfaction and a general happiness about your life, chances are you are on that path. Of course, the opposite of that is probably also true.

Self-Coaching Versus Engaging in a Group Process

This workbook is the first interactive supplement to the book *Freedom To Change,* which provides detailed explanations of many concepts and ideas about our innate freedom to change whatever *we* control in life and want to change. The term "interactive" means that the workbook and its journal components can be utilized by an individual working alone, or by sharing responses with others within a group designed to provide assistance. When working alone, we suggest you think of the process as a type of "Self-Coaching," which implies that a part of you serves as a mentor or life coach for your decisions and actions. That part of you—your mentor—has been defined in the book as your "True Self"—or simply as *the person you are striving to be.* When you become your True Self, you will eventually find yourself on your True Path. When faced with decisions, either decisions that require a lot of thought and deliberation or those that are more spur-of-the-moment, think about the values and ethics that your higher, true self aspires to. Try to act in accordance with what the person you are striving to be would do.

Your higher self, or true self, is your mentor when you work alone. That is what we mean by the term "self-coaching." Let the whisperings and aspirations of your true self guide you.

However, from time to time, we ask that you confer with a few trusted friends about some of the ideas in this process, especially if you are working on this alone.

While you can certainly engage in this process alone, this workbook is ideally utilized within small groups where you will share your responses, hear other people's responses to the same questions and exercises, and interact with them during the group. The group discussions are about sharing, understanding, encouragement, and support—not criticism or condemnation. A life coach, counselor, or other person can be the facilitator of such groups. The group process is the method that is highly recommended to achieve maximum program effectiveness. If you participate in a group, we ask that you follow the instructions and rules of your group and listen to the program facilitator. There will be a few rules and guidelines for all participants that outline the expectations and procedures. Ideally, in the group process, you would meet once a week and review the exercises you did over the past week.

Recommendation—One Set of Written Tasks or Exercises Per Day

This workbook consists of 30 simple exercises and is designed to be completed in a month or so. However, you should *work at your own pace*. While this is designed as a 30-day process, in reality the speed at which you will progress is up to you. In essence, what this workbook represents is a template for people to make choices and gain control over their lives. It is designed to take you into a unique experience of yourself.

Of course, you can do more than one exercise per day, but you may need a bit of time between each exercise to allow it to sink in and have its desired effect. Ultimately, that is up to you. Occasionally, a day's exercise is only a single question, and the very first exercise asks you to write only a single word! On other days, the exercises are a series of tasks, questions, or drawing exercises. When you encounter a "Journal" section, it means that we recommend you don't do more exercises that particular day, but write a bit on the journal pages later or the next morning. It is helpful if you first read the book *Freedom To Change*; however, that isn't a requirement for using this workbook.

Privacy

We recommend that you keep your workbook private. Of course, if you are participating with others, or conferring with trusted friends, you will share some responses, but only the ones you are comfortable with sharing. In addition, we have one other strong recommendation, but ultimately the decision about following it is up to you. *We recommend that you not write anything in your workbook that you don't want others to know.*

Journaling

One component of this workbook, mentioned above, is journaling, where you should make notes to yourself or write down questions that you can ask others as you progress through the program. If you are "into" dreams, by all means write them down in the journal sections. You can also make notes to yourself about health or personal issues as you move through the workbook. You will have a lot of ideas and questions that will emerge along the way, and it's smart to write them down as they will likely be lost in the fog of memory and life's distractions. If you are participating in a group, you can ask questions of other group members or your group facilitator about things you wrote in your journal notes. If you are working alone, you should discuss your questions and comments with a trusted friend.

We highly suggest that you take time to journal each day, as this will encourage you to think more deeply about the exercises. Because each section is designed to last 30 days, there are ample spaces provided after each exercise for journaling. Keep in mind our recommendation that you should not write anything here that you wish to keep completely private.

Drawing

From time to time we'll ask you to make a drawing. These can be as simple as you want or as elaborate as you please. It's up to you, but we ask that you make the drawings by hand with a pencil. Doing the drawings on paper, rather than on a computer, will engage more areas of the brain. You will also find some simple illustrations throughout the workbook, and these can be colored if you like. Coloring is a mindfulness exercise and it helps to clear your thoughts.

The Experience

The Experience is about getting into the present moment in a way that allows you to gain an understanding of your current path in life. You are here, and maybe you aren't sure how or why you got here. Maybe you think that the road you took through life was a series of random coincidences where you made a choice that led you to more random possibilities that presented themselves. In addition, you are perhaps much less certain where your present path is leading. We want you to understand that this is up to you. This is a starting point, but the truth is that every single moment is a starting point.

EXERCISE 1:
WORD

This exercise relates to where you are right now and how various factors in your life have created you, as you are in this moment. It is as simple as it gets. When you have answered the simple questions asked, just let it go and write in the journal section sometime during the remainder of the day.

a. Take your time here, and think about this before answering. Begin by describing yourself in one—and only one—word: _____

b. Next, provide a definition of the one word you chose above to describe yourself. You can use your own definition or take a look at a dictionary to find a formal definition, if it fits:

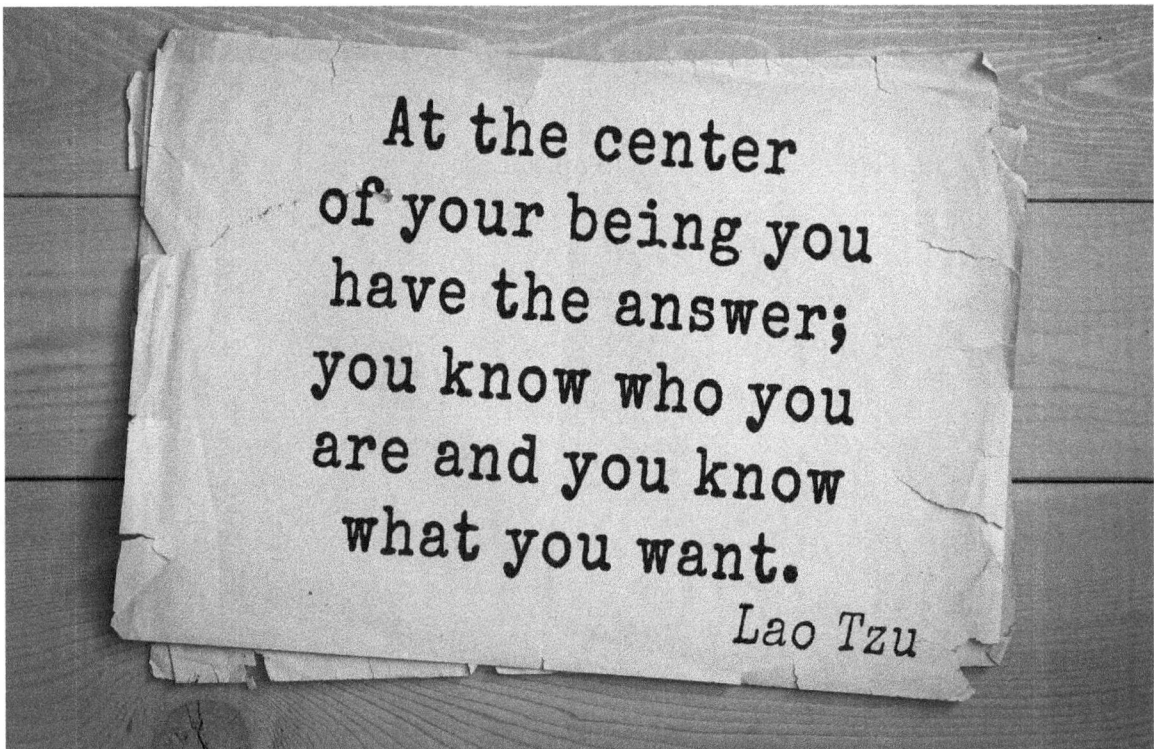

_____

_____

_____

> At the center of your being you have the answer; you know who you are and you know what you want.
>
> Lao Tzu

Daily Journal

_____

_____

_____

_____

_____

_____

_____

_____

_____

_____

_____

_____

EXERCISE 2:
WHY WE ARE THE WAY WE ARE

As explained in the primary *Freedom To Change* book, you are where you are, and the way you are, because of three factors:

1. When you came into this world, you had a set of characteristics and predispositions that were bestowed upon you through genetics and heredity. *To a great extent, your physical attributes, some emotional patterns, and certain personality characteristics are directly influenced by heredity.*

2. The circumstances and environment you were born into and which you grew up in greatly influenced how your genetic predispositions unfolded as well as shaped what you have come to believe about the world and yourself. *In brief, you were influenced by external factors like your family, neighborhood, schooling, and friends to develop in certain ways and to believe in certain things.*

3. Throughout your life, you have made countless choices and decisions that have led you to this exact point in time. *Each choice you made led you step-by-step through a path in life that brought you, ultimately, to this moment in time and to this place.*

   a. To begin the exercises for Day 2, try to think of anything that might have been a hereditary or genetic influence that played a role in *how you came to describe yourself in the one word* you wrote for Exercise 1. Think about your looks, physical attributes, innate intelligence, etc. Some of the things you might consider are the various research findings we presented in the main book. For example, how others react to us is greatly related to our physical appearance. Certain athletic ability and skills are greatly influenced by heredity. Try to think of as many of these as possible and list them below, but keep them focused on that one-word description of yourself you listed in Exercise 1.

   _____

   _____

   _____

   _____

6

b. Now, think about the environment you entered when you were born and consider how these things might have influenced the one word you used to describe yourself in Exercise 1. These things relate to your early life—the people, places, and things that were present during the time when you grew up. Think about the people who raised you and the people you spent time with. How do you think these people, places, and interactions helped shape your one-word description of yourself?

_____

_____

_____

_____

c. Finally, you made choices—countless choices throughout life. Can you list just 5 choices you made in life that impacted the road you chose and that have led you to right now, the present moment, keeping in mind the one word you used in Exercise 1? List them below.

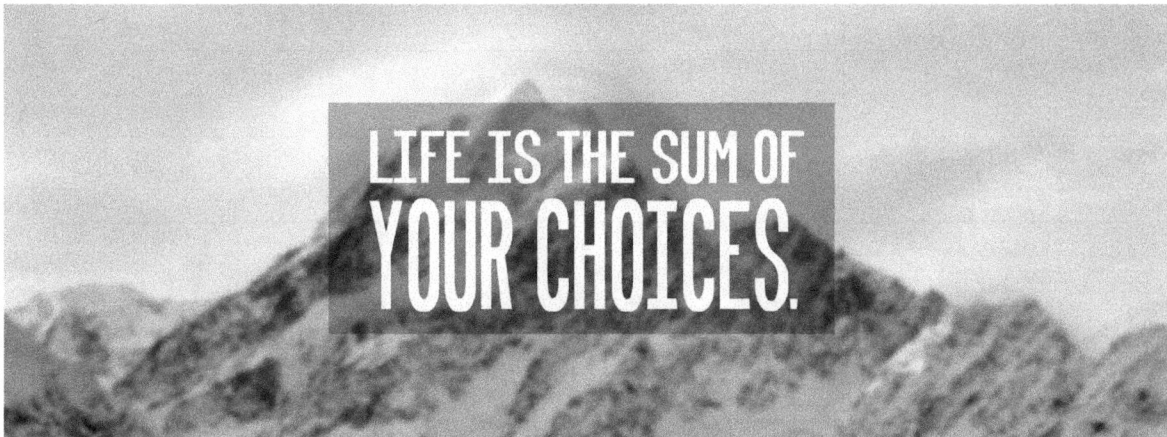

_____

_____

_____

_____

LIFE IS THE SUM OF
YOUR CHOICES.

Daily Journal

EXERCISE 3:
HEREDITY

When you came into this world, you had a set of characteristics and predispositions that were bestowed upon you through genetics and heredity. *To a great extent, your physical attributes, certain emotional patterns, and certain personality characteristics are directly influenced by heredity.*

a. Try to list as many characteristics about yourself that you think were greatly influenced by your heredity. Heredity includes basic looks, body characteristics, innate intelligence, natural athletic abilities, and various other influences.

_____

_____

_____

_____

_____

b. From your list above, can you pick two or three of those characteristics that you know you have the power to change for the better? List them below.

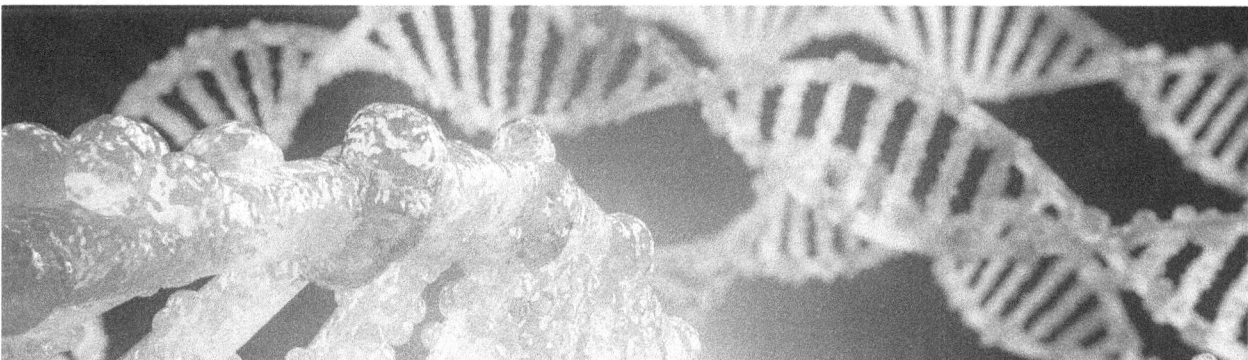

_____

_____

Daily Journal

_____

_____

_____

_____

_____

_____

_____

_____

_____

_____

_____

_____

EXERCISE 4: ENVIRONMENT

The circumstances and environment you were born into and which you grew up in greatly influenced how your genetic predispositions unfolded as well as shaped what you have come to believe about the world and yourself. *You were influenced by your family, neighborhood, schooling, and friends to develop in certain ways and to believe certain things.*

a. Try to think about your personality characteristics, your beliefs, and any habits that were greatly influenced by the factors described in the paragraph above and list them below.

_____

_____

_____

_____

_____

b. From your list above, can you pick two or three of these that you know you can change for the better?

_____

_____

_____

Daily Journal

EXERCISE 5:
CHOICES

Throughout your life, you made countless choices and decisions that have led you to this exact point in time. *Each choice you made led you step-by-step through a path in life that led you, ultimately, to this moment in time and to this place.*

a. Try to think about the choices in your life that led you to this point. Can you list a few of these that you believe were good choices?

_____

_____

_____

_____

b. From the "good choices" you listed above, list a couple that you later enhanced by making new and even better decisions.

_____

_____

_____

_____

Daily Journal

_____

_____

_____

_____

_____

_____

_____

_____

_____

_____

_____

_____

_____

EXERCISE 6:
GOALS

One of the key factors that distinguishes successful people from those who feel unsuccessful is that successful people have usually created a series of goals they wish to achieve as they move through life. Goals can provide motivation and guidance for us as we move along our path in life. Goals give us a type of personal accountability and assist us in using time productively. Goals help us focus ourselves and can be a way for us to measure our progress and overcome obstacles. Setting appropriate goals is definitely one of the hallmarks of the majority of successful people. To start this exercise, we want you to think about three different types of goals you can set, or may have already set, for yourself. These are: 1) Goals related to your health; 2) Goals related to your job, career, or education; 3) Goals related to relationships/family.

a. Start below by listing the goals you have that are related to your health. These can be about exercise, your eating/drinking habits, physical conditions, aging issues, physical appearance, or anything else that is related to health.

_____

_____

_____

_____

b. Next, list several goals that are related to your job, career, or education.

_____

_____

_____

_____

c.   Now, list a few goals that are related to the relationships in your life.

_____

_____

_____

_____

_____

d.   Finally, pick at least one goal from each of the three lists above that you are willing to work on during the time you utilize this workbook.

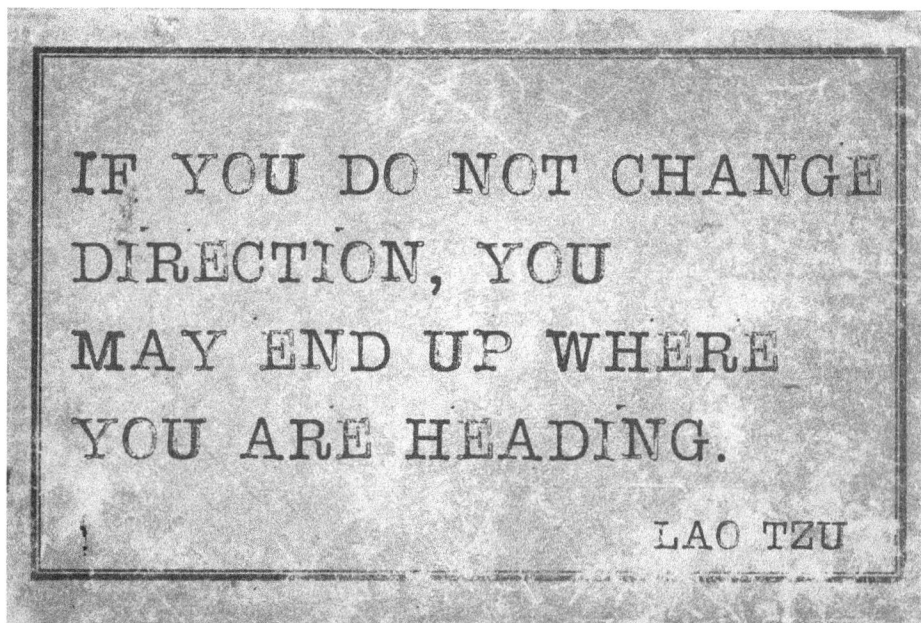

_____

_____

_____

_____

_____

IF YOU DO NOT CHANGE
DIRECTION, YOU
MAY END UP WHERE
YOU ARE HEADING.

LAO TZU

Daily Journal

EXERCISE 7:
GOALS REFINED

There is three errers in this sentence.
Find them.

Chances are that you have seen this riddle before and you already know the answer. But for those who don't know, here is the answer. 1) First, the word "is" should be the plural "are." 2) Obviously the word "errers" is misspelled. 3) Finally, the sentence itself is an error, since there are only two mistakes in it. We use this as a way to show how we are sometimes mentally blocked to only see very obvious things. Due to our underlying beliefs and the way we evaluate things, very few people immediately know the answer to the riddle when it is first presented. Our beliefs can cloud how we see reality and can mask what we call "True Truth." In *Freedom to Change*, we defined true truth by using Meredith Atwood's definition. That definition is: "when you come to the place of honesty with yourself where you have stripped away all the excuses, lies, and blame, revealing the changes and actions you must take to live the optimal life that you truly deserve."

True truth can be difficult to discover and even more difficult to accept. Humans have a tendency to make excuses, blame others, blame circumstances, and we lie, even if it is self-deception. We believe that just about everyone is trying to become someone better than they are right now. However, self-deception, excuses, and blame keep us from changing for the better. These behaviors account for one type of barrier to making a change.

To fulfill important goals, you have to attain *your* true truth. All of us have excuses; we blame others who seem to be obstacles on our path; and yes, we do lie to ourselves—often unconsciously. The true truth is that our goals in life are up to us as individuals. Other people and situations can get in the way of us fulfilling our goals, but in general, these are situations that we can survive, move around, and pass by if we are willing to take the time and make the effort required. The fulfillment of your goals is ultimately up to you, not anyone else. The important thing to remember is that you have to really be devoted to achieving them. All big goals, like getting a college degree, take a lot of work and effort and are actually composed of many smaller goals. We have to remember that we are neurologically wired in a such a way that we tend to avoid things that require times of discomfort or lack of pleasure. We seek to feel good and want to avoid all things that we experience as uncomfortable. Changing is often uncomfortable and often requires sustained effort. In *Freedom To Change*, we mentioned several times that we are programmed to follow the path of least resistance. That means we often take the easiest path now rather than the more difficult one that will potentially lead to the greatest reward in the future.

As the final exercise at this point, the end of your first week, we ask you to take a good look at the goals you set for yourself in your Day 6 exercises. Once you have these in mind, answer the following questions.

a.   Why do you want to achieve each goal?

_____

_____

_____

_____

_____

_____

_____

_____

_____

_____

_____

_____

_____

b. How will each goal help you become happier or more satisfied?

_____

_____

_____

_____

_____

_____

_____

_____

c. How much time will each goal take to achieve?

_____

_____

_____

_____

_____

_____

_____

_____

d. Are you willing to do the work required to achieve each goal?_____

Daily Journal

EXERCISE 8:
REVISITING THE WORD

Quickly count the number of "f's" (the letter f or F) in the following sentence.

Federal Fuses are the result of years of scientific study combined with the experience of many.

Your answer: _____

(The answer is on page 37.)

Let's start this new week by revisiting the one-word answer you used to describe yourself back in Exercise 1. Do you think that the one word you used then to describe yourself is still accurate? Your answer really doesn't matter, but let's try a little experiment with it.

a. In the space that follows, write the word again: _____

b. Now, try to think of a reason why it is not always true. This task is easier than you probably think. Let's say you wrote the word *happy*. There's a good chance that you aren't always or continually happy. You can certainly think of a time when you were not happy, were bored, or were exhausted. If you used the word *honest* to describe yourself, we are fairly certain you can think of a time when you were not completely honest. The same logic applies to nearly any word you might use to describe your-self. Humans are complex beings, and life changes—as do our moods and feelings. So, why is the word you used not always true?

_____

_____

_____

_____

_____

c. Now, try to think of one—and only one—word, that best describes you today:

_____

Daily Journal

_____

_____

_____

_____

_____

_____

_____

_____

_____

_____

_____

_____

_____

_____

EXERCISE 9: SMART GOALS

In your exercises for Day 6, you listed three goals that you believe you can work on during your time participating in this workbook. This exercise takes a closer look at them.

Life coaches use what is known as the SMART method of setting goals. The words comprising the acronym SMART are sometimes defined as *specific, measurable, achievable, relevant, and timely*. As shown in the illustration below, there are also some variations that are used.

S specific
strategic
significant

M measurable
meaningful
motivational

A attainable
achievable
adjustable

R relevant
realistic
results

T timely
tractable
tangible

Goal setting

a. Begin by relisting your three goals from exercise 6 on the lines below. **Note: If you want to change any of them, now is a good time to do it.** After you list them, take a look at each goal using the SMART method. Below each goal, determine if it is *specific, measurable, achievable, relevant, and timely*. A goal is specific if it is easily understood by anyone. It is measurable if there is a clear way to determine if it has been completed. It is achievable if it is under your control and is truly possible. A relevant goal is one that has some genuine importance to you. Timely means that you have a realistic timeframe established for achieving it.

Goal 1:

a. Is it specific? _____

b. Can it be measured? _____

c. Is it achievable? _____

d. Is it relevant and important? _____

e. Do you have a realistic timeframe? _____

Goal 2:

a. Is it specific? _____

b. Can it be measured? _____

c. Is it achievable? _____

d. Is it relevant and important? _____

e. Do you have a realistic timeframe? _____

Goal 3:

a. Is it specific? _____

b. Can it be measured? _____

c. Is it achievable? _____

d. Is it relevant and important? _____

e. Do you have a realistic timeframe? _____

Daily Journal

_____

_____

_____

_____

_____

_____

_____

_____

_____

_____

_____

_____

EXERCISE 10: THE FIRST THING

In the last exercise, you wrote down three goals. Today, we'll ask something simple. Start by relisting the goals. Then, below each one, answer the three questions.

Goal 1:

a. What is the first thing you need to do to begin the process of achieving this goal?

_____

b. Have you started? _____

c. If not, when will you start? _____

Goal 2:

a. What is the first thing you need to do to begin the process of achieving this goal?

_____

b. Have you started? _____

c. If not, when will you start? _____

Goal 3:

a. What is the first thing you need to do to begin the process of achieving this goal?

_____

b. Have you started? _____

c. If not, when will you start? _____

Daily Journal

_____

_____

_____

_____

_____

_____

_____

_____

_____

_____

_____

_____

_____

_____

EXERCISE 11:
THE THREE TRUTHS

In *Freedom To Change* we presented three big truths about life. These were that humans have three primary drives built into us that seemingly impact everything we do. These are: 1) The will to survive; 2) The drive to reproduce and preserve our species; and 3) A relentless drive to make life easier and as pleasurable as possible. In essence, both of the last two drives (reproduction and making life easier and more pleasurable) serve the survival drive in one way or another.

We are sure that some people will disagree with the ideas in the above paragraph. Perhaps you are one of those people. So, as a brief mental exercise, try to bring to mind some of the important things in your life. Think about what you do with your time. Pause for a moment here and think about a typical day in your life. Think about the people you interact with. You can think about your job, daily duties, and any routines you might have.

a. After considering the various things, events, people, and routines that make up your life, try to think of the things you do that **do not** somehow relate to survival, reproduction and preservation of life, or things that make life easier and more enjoyable. What in your life does not somehow relate to those three forces that drive our behavior? Write them below:

_____

_____

_____

b. Some people won't be able to think of anything at all. However, if you have written something above, think about what that behavior or activity serves to do. In the space below, try to answer this: What is the goal of that behavior or activity?

_____

_____

_____

_____

c. If you were unable to think of anything you do that **does not** relate to those three drives we mentioned above, answer this question. What do you think it means to you with respect to the decisions you make in life?

_____

_____

_____

_____

d. Finally, think about this idea for a moment. Most of our habits form because of the will to survive and to make life easier and more pleasurable. However, it is also true that some of our habits can become unhealthy. The things we eat, what we drink, and the physical activities we do or do not engage in can all lead to the development of unhealthy habits. If that is true for you, can you think of ways that you can manage or change any bad habits you have?

_____

_____

_____

_____

_____

_____

Daily Journal

_____

_____

_____

_____

_____

_____

_____

_____

_____

_____

_____

_____

_____

EXERCISE 12: MEANING OF LIFE

In *Freedom To Change*, we presented an idea about the meaning of life. It is a simple and practical definition. *It is that your meaning of life is whatever you make it to be.* That leaves a vast number of possibilities. You can make your life about anything you desire: Pleasure, power, sex, family, work, money, spirituality, taking, or giving. It's up to you. For some people, all they do is try to make it through a day. At least for that day, that's their meaning in life. Also, we asserted that the meaning of life changes over the course of a lifetime. One's meaning at age 4 is different than when that person turns 21, and our meaning of life continues to change quite a bit as we age. We also believe that an individual's meaning can be discerned from what he or she does and how that person leads his or her life. What this means is if you could really see what a person does consistently over time, you'd get a fair idea of that person's meaning of life.

a. Is this something you agree with? _____

b. Why or why not? _____

_____

c. If an outsider observed what you typically do in life, what would that person say is your meaning of life? _____

_____

_____

d. What do *you* say your meaning of life is? _____

_____

_____

e. Is there a difference between the answers you gave in c & d? _____

f. If there is a difference, does that difference mean anything important to you?

_____

_____

_____

Daily Journal

EXERCISE 13: SAFETY AND SECURITY

In the 1960s, psychologist Abraham Maslow theorized that humans go through a series of stages in life where we tend to focus on fulfilling increasingly complex needs. The most basic stage of all is the need for safety and security as well as having the things we need for survival. From that basic level, we progress through stages where we meet various psychological needs and then on to issues that relate to our self-esteem and fulfillment in life. The figure below depicts a typical representation of Maslow's Hierarchy of Needs.

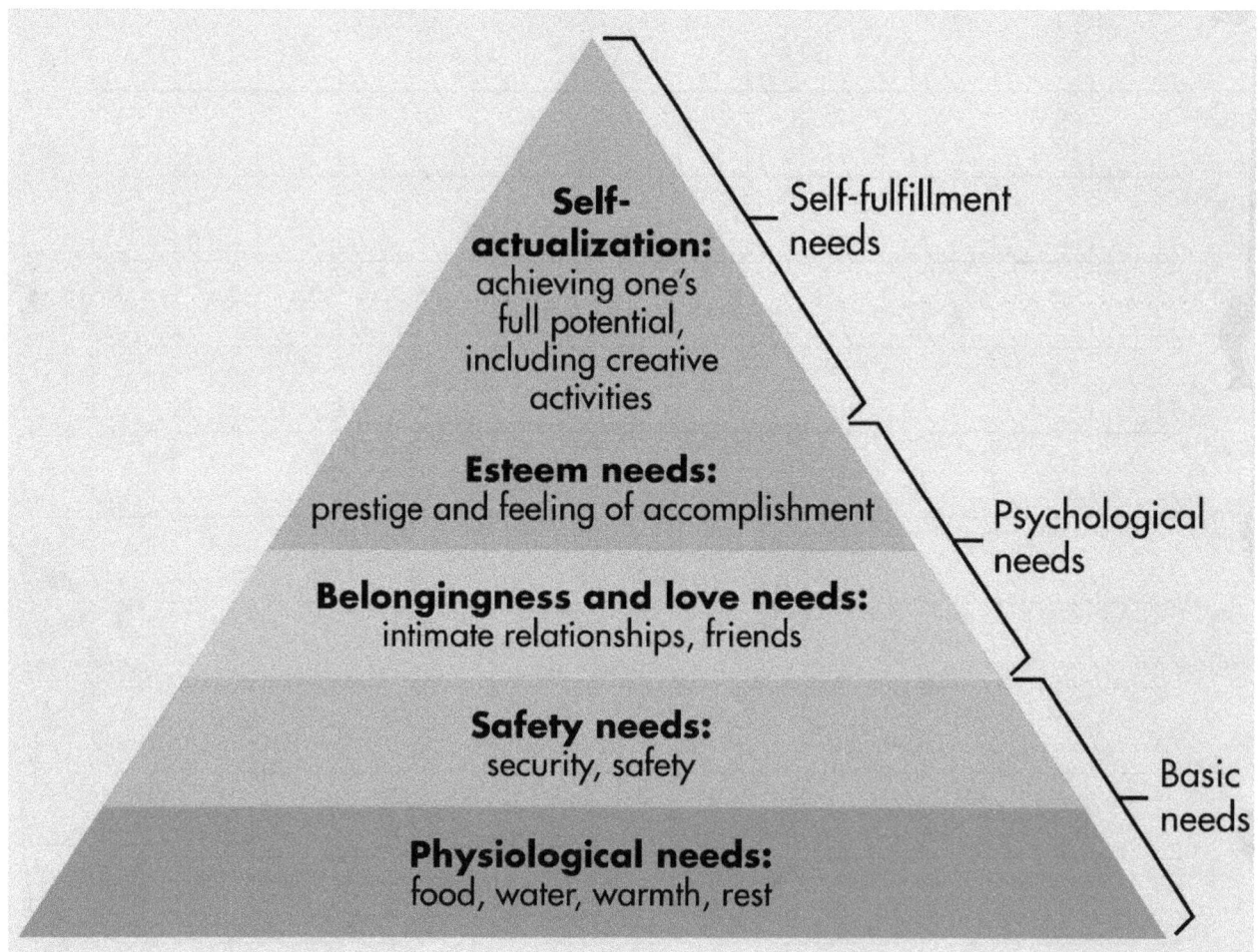

Self-fulfillment needs

Self-actualization: achieving one's full potential, including creative activities

Esteem needs: prestige and feeling of accomplishment

Psychological needs

Belongingness and love needs: intimate relationships, friends

Safety needs: security, safety

Basic needs

Physiological needs: food, water, warmth, rest

a. Study the figure on the previous page and try to determine where you are right now. If you have your basic needs met—those things that relate to having sufficient food and safety—chances are that you are working on higher levels. Where do you see yourself now, based on Maslow's levels?

_____

_____

_____

_____

b. The level of safety and security usually encompasses financial issues as well as things like debt, the ability to consistently pay it off, having sufficient insurance, and overall feelings of having sufficient resources. No matter how much higher we progress on Maslow's stages, we always keep an eye on maintaining that safety and security level. With the understanding that safety and security issues are always influencing us, do you feel as if you have basically fulfilled that level and are living in the levels above it?

_____

_____

_____

_____

Daily Journal

_____

_____

_____

_____

_____

_____

_____

_____

_____

_____

_____

_____

EXERCISE 14:
GOALS SERVING OUR NEEDS

"Federal Fuses are the result of years of scientific study
combined with the experience of many."

How many "f's" are in that sentence?_____

There are six "f's" in the sentence above. If you got it right, kudos to you. If you got less than six, you didn't see the three times the word "of" was used. In life, we can easily miss obvious, but important, little things when we are focused on the bigger picture of our life. There is an old saying, "The devil is in the details." Most goals have smaller goals linked to them. Those small goals are essentially details, and if they aren't done, the big goal will get lost. Often that's where we employ self-deception, place blame, and make excuses. The devil is in the details. Let's return to Maslow's theory for a moment and do something a little unusual.

a. Start below by relisting the three goals you set for yourself in exercises 9 and 10.

   1. _____

   2. _____

   3. _____

b. Now, let's go back to Maslow's hierarchy. Refer back to page 34. Take a moment and examine each goal you wrote above. Then try to determine which of Maslow's level of needs that each of your 3 goals serves. For example, if one goal is to obtain a better home in a safer neighborhood, it is likely motivated by safety and security. If a goal pertains to improving a love relationship, the goal likely fits on Maslow's level of love, belonging, and relationships. *Next to each goal you wrote above, write down the "need" level from Maslow's hierarchy* that you determined is probably motivating the goal.

c. Do you see a pattern in the level or levels that your goals are coming from? _____

d. If you see a pattern, what does it mean to you? _____

_____

_____

_____

Daily Journal

_____

_____

_____

_____

_____

_____

_____

_____

_____

_____

_____

_____

_____

EXERCISE 15:
TWO BIG RULES FOR DECISIONS

There is a clever riddle that many people have heard at one time or another. If you have heard it, that's okay. But here is one variation of it.

> *You are trapped in a room that has only two doors. One door leads to freedom and the other leads to doom. You want to go through the freedom door. You have to decide which door is the one to freedom, and you have some help because there is a guard stationed at each door. One of them always tells a lie and the other always tells the truth, but you don't know which one is the liar and which one tells the truth. You are allowed to ask one—and only one—question. And you can ask that question to one—and only one—guard. What is the question you ask to determine the door to freedom, and which guard do you ask?*
>
> *(The answer is on page 60.)*

(The answer is on page 60.)

There are two big rules we believe should always be taken into consideration when you make any decision. **These are: 1) First, do no harm; 2) Then do the best you can with the resources available to you.** These two rules come from medicine and various helping professions. But we believe they provide a simple and good guideline for all decision-making. The idea behind "Do no harm" is a good one, but life can be filled with complicated decisions where the choice can help one person and also seemingly be detrimental to others. In addition, we seldom have all the facts of a given situation. The second guideline assists us in complicated situations. You can choose to do the best you can with all the resources that are available to you. The same rule applies to decisions we make that impact us personally. You are generally advised to do no harm but do the best you can. Sometimes there is time to gather the information needed, but we don't always avail ourselves of the opportunity to find out what the best choices are. And sometimes we don't have perfect choices. In fact, life seldom presents us with the perfect choice. So, do the best you can with what you have.

We have used several exercises to discuss goals but haven't really gone into depth about them. So let's look at a very common goal from the perspective of the two rules outlined above. Lots of people want to lose weight. Unfortunately, too many people set unreasonable goals with respect to losing weight. We won't get into the complicated details here, but a 2000 book entitled *It Can Break Your Heart* (Milnor, Little, & Robinson), explains that it is an unreasonable goal to expect to lose more than 3.5 pounds of fat per week, and even that can be very unreasonable for the vast majority of people over any extended period of time. Body fat can be added pretty quickly, but taking it off takes a lot more time and a type of endurance that requires an enormous amount of discipline and willpower. The drive to avoid discomfort and seek pleasure can get in the way of weight loss efforts. It's built into us with a mixture of hormones and brain areas screaming at us to eat what feels good.

The fact is that the vast majority of people who attempt to lose weight usually put it all back on soon after their efforts wane. The result is what is referred to as yo-yo dieting that can also involve alternating periods of intense "exercise" followed by a collapse of sorts, leading to inactivity. Understand that we are not saying that losing weight isn't a good goal—what we are saying is that the goal has to be reasonable and smart. Effective weight loss does not happen overnight. You have to take time to gather the relevant information. You don't want to do harm to yourself, and you want to do the best you can with the resources available to you. With a goal like losing weight, slow and steady progress builds good habits over the long term. On the other hand, setting unreasonable and unattainable goals can do harm and does not involve using all of the resources that are available to you. With the weight loss goal, you don't want to create a bad habit like yo-yo dieting. In addition, there are lots of resources available that can help you determine a reasonable plan of action and help you understand what is really possible. Now, let's apply this to your own goals.

a. Start below by relisting the three goals you set for yourself a few exercises ago. If you have seen that you need to change the goals, that's okay.

1. _____

2. _____

3. _____

b. Next, for each goal, answer the questions below.

Goal 1:

1. Can you see any way that setting (or trying to achieve) this goal could do harm to

   you or others? _____

2. Have you identified all of the resources necessary for you to achieve this goal?

   _____

3. Are you willing to choose the right resources and utilize them?_____

Goal 2:

1. Can you see any way that setting (or trying to achieve) this goal could do harm to you or others? _____

2. Have you identified all of the resources necessary for you to achieve this goal?

   _____

3. Are you willing to choose the right resources and utilize them?_____

Goal 3:

1. Can you see any way that setting (or trying to achieve) this goal could do harm to you or others? _____

2. Have you identified all of the resources necessary for you to achieve this goal?

   _____

3. Are you willing to choose the right resources and utilize them?_____

SOMETIMES, THE HARDEST THING AND THE RIGHT THING ARE THE SAME.

Daily Journal

EXERCISE 16: NEVER-ENDING PLEASURE

Back in Exercise 11, we talked about three truths in human nature. One of those truths is that we typically strive to make life easier and more pleasurable. That's a natural and normal thing for us to do. But can it go too far? You already know the answer to that question. Countless books and movies have addressed this question. In philosopher Robert Nozick's 1974 book *Anarchy, State, and Utopia*, the question was raised about how pleasure-seeking humans are and what we would do if faced with what is a probable reality that looms in our not-so-distant future? The idea Nozick proposed is somewhat similar to the simulated reality in the movie *The Matrix*. We'll paraphrase what Nozick wrote in 1974:

Imagine that a computer simulation device existed that was able to provide you with any type of reality experience you wanted for an indefinite period of time—even for your entire lifetime. You would be hooked up to the device and kept alive for a normal lifetime—and what you experienced in your brain would appear to you just as real as the reality you live in now. You would be totally unaware of the condition of your actual body (which lies dormant in suspended animation), and you would be mentally living in this adaptive computer-produced reality. In brief, the experience you would have would be well beyond what we now call "virtual reality." It would become your reality, indistinguishable from the "real" world. You would feel, taste, smell, move, and hear everything in that reality exactly as you do now in the real world. The difference is that you could choose anything and everything that happens in that reality. You could look any way you wanted, be with anyone you wanted, and do whatever you wanted. You could be in any job, career, sport, or anything else you choose. How many people would choose to do it? Would you?

a. What would the advantages be if people could live in this virtual world where they could be and do whatever they wanted?

_____

_____

_____

_____

_____

43

b. What percentage of the American population do you think might be willing to live in the way described in the computer simulation example?

_____

c. What would happen to society if the above became commonplace?

_____

_____

_____

_____

_____

d. What do you think might happen to you if you did what is described above?

_____

_____

_____

_____

_____

e. If you did place yourself in this situation, how would you describe the meaning of life to others?

_____

_____

_____

_____

f.　Do you think that your current use of digital devices is in any way leading you toward that path?

_____

_____

_____

_____

_____

_____

Daily Journal

_____

_____

_____

_____

_____

_____

_____

_____

_____

_____

_____

_____

_____

_____

EXERCISE 17: CONSTANT PLEASURE AS A PROBLEM

In *Freedom To Change,* we mentioned two factors that relate to the drive we have to make life as easy and as enjoyable as possible. Those are: 1) We tend to follow the path of least resistance; and 2) Our unconscious makes many of our choices for us automatically.

The *path of least resistance* means we are programmed to take the easiest and most pleasurable path—or the least painful one—when faced with choices. It doesn't happen with everything we do, but it's still present in just about everyone's life. Lots of research has shown this strong human tendency is very real. The path of least resistance seldom requires much thought. For the person trying to lose weight, the path of least resistance is doing nothing different today and thinking, "Tomorrow I'll start." Often this occurs unconsciously, and automatic habitual eating habits kick in. In essence, the pleasure or easy life we can have in the moment can override what we envision or hope for in the future. It might be accurate to say that "doing nothing different" is often the result of taking the path of least resistance.

The idea of the unconscious making decisions without us actually being aware of it can be a bit tricky. Of course, it doesn't happen all the time, but it does happen. Research has shown that when we are faced with certain types of situations and different choices in them, we often decide on a level below our conscious awareness. There are parts of the brain that get engaged quickly and they make decisions automatically before we even know we have decided. We are sure you can think of times where you reacted to a situation quickly and said or did something you really didn't intend, or at least you wish you hadn't reacted so quickly. If you had time to think about it, you might have reacted differently. Research has pointed out that deep within our brain, some situations are processed so quickly that we aren't aware of it happening. It is a survival mechanism that has become so forceful that it takes over. Then we react, and because we often react before we make conscious or thoughtful decisions, the reactions are, by definition, unconscious. So, where do these unconscious reactions come from in the brain? Without going into depth here, let's just say they come from your beliefs and habits. Consider the "automatic habitual eating habits" we mentioned in the previous paragraph. When you watch television or go to a movie, the unconscious has programmed you to eat the things you usually do in that circumstance. The unconscious has primed us to respond to nearly everything.

a. Can you think of a time when you made an important decision so quickly that you were surprised?

_____

_____

b. Why do you think it happened that way?

_____

_____

_____

_____

_____

c. Have you ever made a quick decision you regretted?

_____

_____

d. Can you think of a few examples where you made a decision simply because it was the easiest thing?

_____

_____

_____

_____

e. With respect to the three goals you set a few exercises ago, do you think the "path of least resistance" can cause you problems in achieving those goals?

_____

_____

_____

_____

Daily Journal

EXERCISE 18: BELIEFS

In *Freedom To Change,* a great deal of attention was placed on beliefs. So let's discuss beliefs a bit, but in a different way. Let's start by defining what *beliefs* are. Beliefs are really your "collection" of thoughts about a topic, situation, person, place, or thing. By using the word collection, we are implying that thoughts about a particular area or topic tend to cluster around each other in an organized way. Beliefs are our way of defining things so that we can quickly assess and deal with situations that might arise. You probably have a set of beliefs about men, women, children, police, work, and various other things or situations. Beliefs can be both effective and efficient ways to deal with reality but they can also be exceedingly restrictive. They can, and usually do, restrict our perceptions and shrink our reality. What does that mean?

In short, unquestioned or unexamined beliefs can limit your life. Beliefs restrict how we perceive reality. The most obvious examples are how we view other races and the opposite sex—or all sexes. Beliefs about yourself restrict you, but they can also help you. You have to know your limitations, right? Your beliefs shape how you experience the world and its events. We all perceive the world in a way that conforms to our own belief system. But things change. Things change not *because* of your beliefs, but *in spite of* them.

a. Which of your beliefs affect the way you dress?

_____

b. Which of your beliefs relate to the things you habitually do?

_____

c. Which of your beliefs relate to your safety and security issues?

_____

d. Which of your beliefs relate to your work or career?

_____

e. Which of your beliefs relate to your health?

_____

f. Which beliefs do you have about something important to you?

_____

g. Which beliefs do you have about the opposite sex, people of another race, people from other countries, or people who participate in other religions?

_____

_____

h. With respect to what you wrote in "f.", which feelings or emotions are attached to the important beliefs you listed?

_____

_____

_____

_____

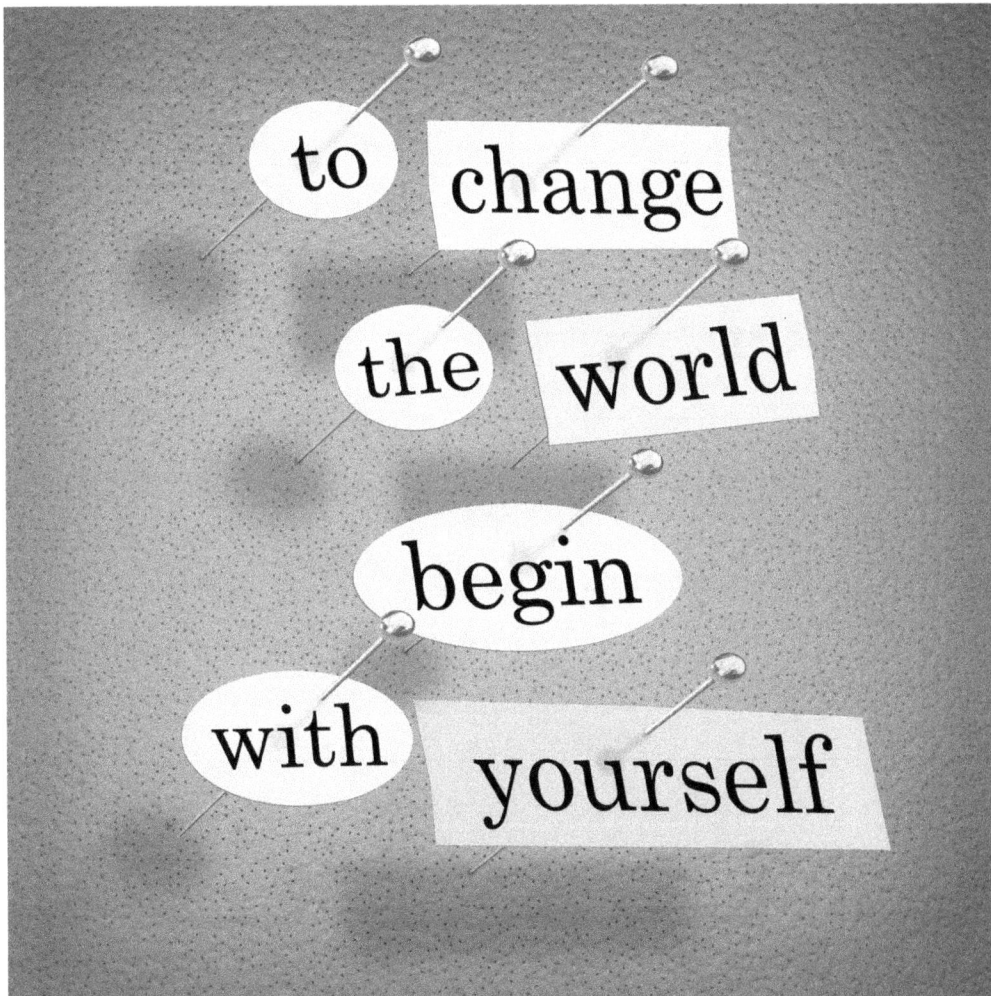

to change the world begin with yourself

Daily Journal

EXERCISE 19: BELIEFS AND FEELINGS

Last exercise we ended with a question about feelings and emotions being attached to beliefs. It is something that most people can easily understand, yet it slips from day-to-day relevance. What that means is the following: We are prisoners of our emotions and reactions... and we are confined by our beliefs—but we are seldom aware of it. Perhaps the most obvious example is how you dress. Your beliefs about yourself restrict and limit the clothes you usually wear. The profound influence beliefs hold over us go far deeper than that though. To understand this, bring to mind some situations where your strongest beliefs were being debated. It might be times when you were discussing politics, religion, science, a particular person, or sports. There are lots of possible examples. Try to think of at least one of these situations where you were in a debate or argument over beliefs about someone or something.

The part of such situations you should really pay attention to is what happened when someone strongly or totally disagreed with you. Chances are that one or both of you involved in the discussion of a strong belief eventually had significant feelings or emotions emerge. Maybe it devolved into an argument or just ended with hurt feelings. The point here is that feelings and emotions are always attached to beliefs, and when the beliefs are stimulated or challenged, that is when feelings and emotions emerge. Keep in mind that we have previously stated that beliefs also serve a useful purpose. Our beliefs organize our world and make us ready to respond. At the same time, however, they can limit us.

Our beliefs serve as our own set of rules. They give us a way to analyze the world quickly without too much thought. We are emotionally invested in these beliefs because they are *our* beliefs. Therein lies the problem. *The emotional investment we have in being right about a belief can far outweigh reason.* Here is a truth that a lot of scientists assert: Almost everything that we believe to be true is, in reality, uncertain. This can be a difficult thing to comprehend. It is even more difficult to disconnect the beliefs from the feelings attached to them. One way to start doing this is to come to understand and accept that anything that is truly a belief is very likely to have an exception—and usually many more than one exception.

a. Think back to a time when you believed something that you eventually realized wasn't true. It doesn't matter what it was, just think of a belief that you changed after realizing that it wasn't accurate. List it below, and if you can, think of more than one.

_____

_____

_____

b. Most people think they are a good judge of other people. Think of a person who did not turn out the way you initially believed he or she was.

_____

c. Write about a job or a task you had that you initially believed was going to turn out a certain way, but it actually went in an opposite direction.

_____

d. Politics is an especially nasty area when it comes to our beliefs and feelings. Can you think of a politician who you really believed was a certain way, but later you realized that you were wrong?

_____

e. Here is your first drawing exercise. Take your time—or do it quickly. It's up to you. You can make it as simple or complex as you want. Draw stick people if you'd like. In the space below, make a drawing of yourself in the center. Then around the drawing of you, draw the important people, key events, and important responsibilities you have. You don't have to draw all of them, just the ones that immediately come to mind. Finally, if you are certain that your book won't fall into the hands of people whom you would rather not see it, write a key belief about each of the people or things you drew around you. Otherwise, just bring to mind a key belief about each.

Daily Journal

_____

_____

_____

_____

_____

_____

_____

_____

_____

_____

_____

_____

_____

_____

_____

_____

EXERCISE 20: BELIEFS THAT LIMIT YOU

All of us have habits. Not just habits like brushing our teeth or the way we dress, but our consistent personality characteristics and the ways in which we treat other people are fundamentally habitual. We do the same things over and over because that's what our beliefs tell us we should do. In short, when we "learn" something, that *something* is typically a belief. Beliefs tell us, "This is how the world is and this is what I need to do." If our responses don't work out, we usually blame anything except our beliefs. What we expect to happen in situations also comes from our beliefs, and when our expectations aren't met, we seldom recognize that our beliefs might be to blame. Another insight is that our beliefs about *what the world is and what it should be* are major contributors to our unhappiness. Our beliefs can oppose reality. They can resist true truth. It is the resistance to reality and the true truth about situations that often cause or worsen our pain and anguish. A key issue in this is that *we want to be right* about our beliefs. We are so driven by *the desire to be right that it can become more important to us than being happy.* Many of us blame others or situations for just about everything that's bad, which wreaks havoc on our relationships. Rather than placing blame, a reassessment of our beliefs is a better approach to resolving unhappiness. It could be said that placing blame is human nature and that we are just wired that way. In general, we try to take credit for the good things that happen. We affirm to ourselves that our belief is right. When things go wrong, we often try to place blame elsewhere. We seldom consider that our beliefs may have been the problem, and instead we confirm to ourselves that our belief is right and the others involved are to blame. But does being right really matter? You have to ask yourself whether being right matters more than your happiness and more than having peace in your relationships?

a. Think about something in your life that went right. You won something; you got something you wanted; or you accomplished something. Write a brief description of the first thing that comes to mind about it below:

_____

_____

_____

_____

_____

b. Look at what you wrote in "a" and think about all the things that happened for that situation to turn out the way you wanted. Was there anything in that situation that was not completely under your control?

_____

_____

_____

_____

c. Obviously you did something to make the situation above work for you. In a few words, describe what you did.

_____

_____

_____

_____

d. When you first encountered the situation above, what were some of your key beliefs?

_____

_____

_____

_____

e. Now think of something in your life that went wrong or just didn't work out. Write a brief description below.

_____

_____

_____

_____

_____

f. What in the situation above was not under your control?

_____

_____

_____

g. What was under your control?

_____

_____

_____

h. When you first encountered the situation above, what were some of your key beliefs?

_____

_____

_____

_____

_____

Daily Journal

_____

_____

_____

_____

_____

_____

_____

_____

_____

_____

_____

_____

_____

_____

_____

_____

_____

EXERCISE 21: UNDERSTANDING CAN BE A USELESS GAME

The answer to the riddle posed at the beginning of Exercise 15 is pretty simple, but it takes logic and a bit of cleverness to figure out. Feelings, emotions, and beliefs about it don't matter. Nor does fairness matter. That was one point in asking you to solve it. Recall that in the riddle you were in a room that had two doors and two guards. One of the guards always lied and the other always told the truth. One door led to freedom and the other door led to doom. You could ask only one question to only one guard about which door led to freedom. If you didn't get the answer to the riddle, here it is. The answer to the question of *which guard* you ask is: *it doesn't matter*. You can ask either guard the same question. It is the *precise question* you ask either guard that matters. There are two variations to that question, but we'll only cite one. The question you would ask either guard is: *"Which door will the **other** guard say is the door to freedom?"* If you asked that question to either guard, that person would point to the door leading to doom. So obviously you'd choose the door either guard does NOT point toward. It's actually simple but lots of people don't easily figure it out. As we stated at the beginning of this paragraph, sometimes feelings, emotions, and beliefs don't matter. In fact, you might have thought at some point in life, "This is stupid and unrealistic," or "It's unfair and ridiculous." Yes. It is. So here is an important point. Over the course of a person's lifetime, he or she will wind up in many ridiculous, unfair, stupid, and unrealistic situations. Your feelings, emotions, or beliefs only matter in those situations if you allow them to matter. And sometimes by using reason and logic, you can work yourself out of such situations.

In Exercise 20, you were asked about two different situations in your life. You were asked to think of something that worked out well for you and a situation that didn't work out. In many areas of life, we take credit for the good that happens and blame something or someone for what goes wrong. Does that really matter? It does, but only if you learn a few simple lessons from it.

One lesson is this. *Understanding can be a useless game.* We can try to understand but we have limits placed on us by our beliefs and other factors. Trying to understand feelings, emotions, and beliefs can muddle things quickly. The reasons things happen as they do can be complicated. The truth is, we can never really understand situations completely and with total awareness. *Understanding doesn't change anything, unless it changes actual behavior.*

Few beliefs are completely and always accurate; if they were totally accurate, they would no longer be beliefs. In fact, we wouldn't refer to them as beliefs. Feelings and emotions are certainly an important part of the human experience and are designed to be that way. We aren't saying that they are unimportant or should be ignored. In fact, you can't really ignore them. What we are saying is that their effects are largely unconscious—meaning they usually emerge outside of your conscious control. As we discussed in detail in *Freedom To Change*, you can delve into your unconscious and try to understand it all, but once you think you understand the unconscious stuff, it eventually submerges back into the unconscious. And then it continues to affect you in ways that escape your awareness. You have only 2 choices in this: 1) Let your unconscious rule you and control you, or 2) Take charge and determine your path.

a. Take a moment and consider the three goals you set for yourself several exercises ago. You remember them, right? At least one of those goals is stuck, or sort of stuck. Maybe all three are. Settle on one goal that's both important to you and also one that you think isn't progressing as you wish. For this exercise, we would like for you to make a few simple drawings in the space provided on the next page. In the center (A), make a drawing of you completing that goal successfully. In the space at the top (B), try to draw or write any beliefs or unconscious issues you think may be impeding you. In the box on the left side (C), draw a picture or write your habits that have impeded you. In the box on the right side (D), draw a picture of the things you need to do in order to complete the goal. In the box at the bottom (E), write out what you hope to gain by fulfilling the goal.

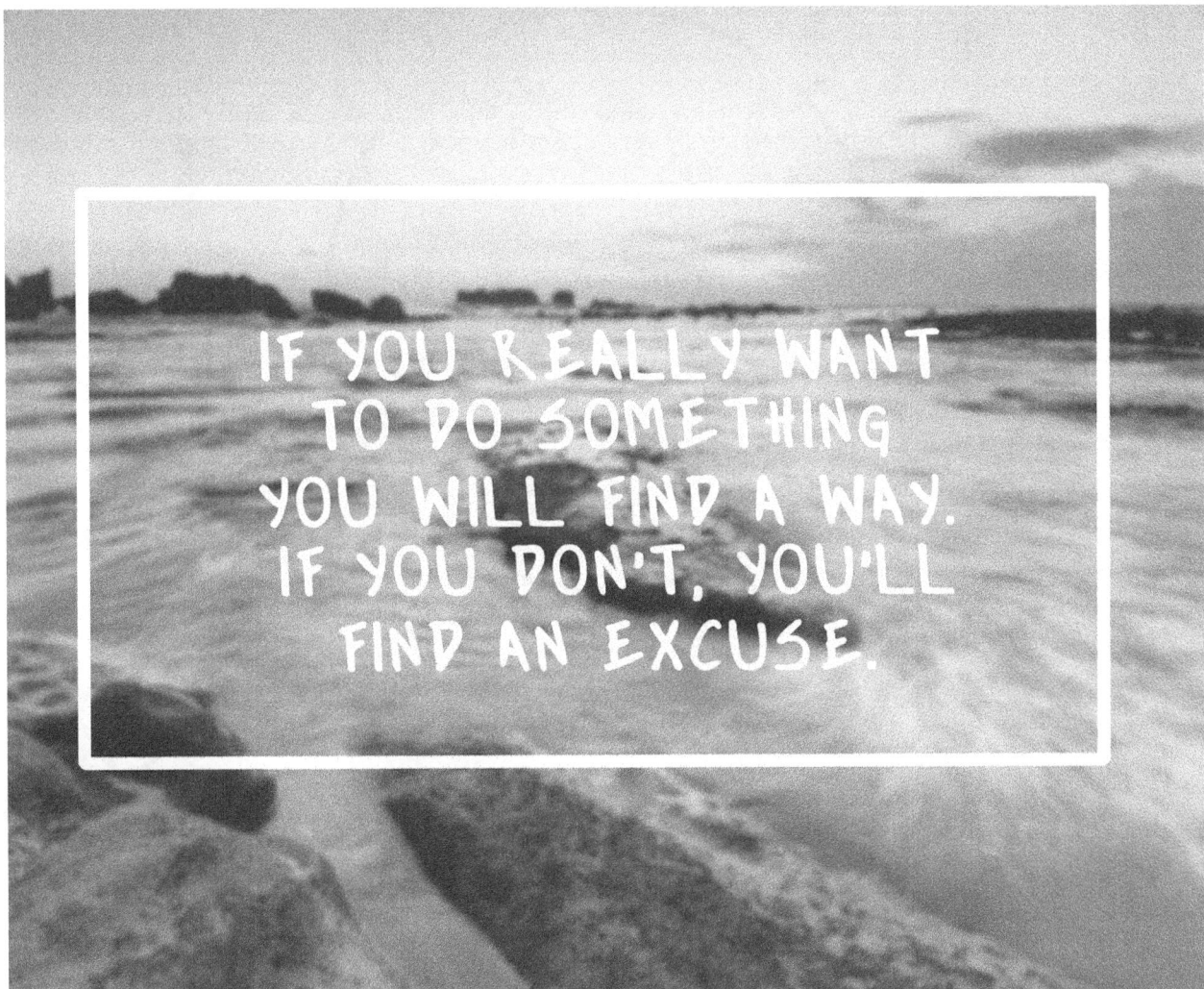

IF YOU REALLY WANT TO DO SOMETHING YOU WILL FIND A WAY. IF YOU DON'T, YOU'LL FIND AN EXCUSE.

(A), make a drawing of you completing that goal successfully. In the space at the top (B), try to draw or write any beliefs or unconscious issues you think may be impeding you. In the box on the left side (C), draw a picture or write your habits that have impeded you. In the box on the right side (D), draw a picture of the things you need to do in order to complete the goal. In the box at the bottom (E), write out what you hope to gain by fulfilling the goal.

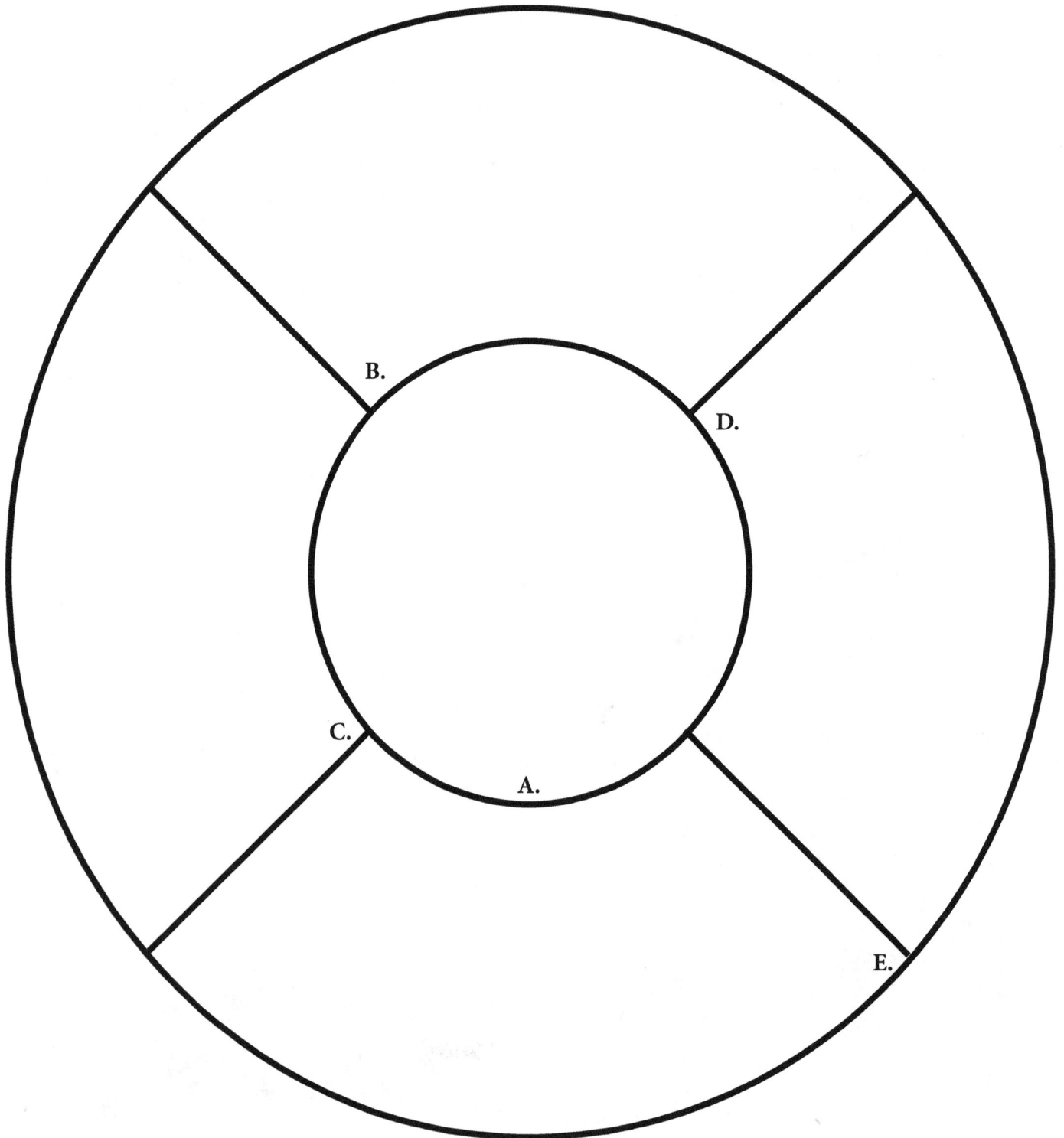

B.

D.

C.

A.

E.

Daily Journal

_____

_____

_____

_____

_____

_____

_____

_____

_____

_____

_____

_____

_____

_____

EXERCISE 22:
BEING WRONG AND CONTROL

Here is a little science question. Pretend that you have a top—one of those children's toys that you can wind up and it spins around and around balanced on a tip at its bottom. Before you spin the top, you lay it on a highly accurate scale that weighs it very precisely and to the smallest degree possible. Then you spin the top on the same scale and weigh it again while it's spinning. The question is: does the top weigh the same when it's not moving as compared to when it's spinning? This is not a trick question. You'll find the answer on page 90.

It might come as a bit of a surprise that we'll say this, but being wrong can be a good thing and can lead a person to truth. Every one of us is wrong about something. We are probably wrong about a whole lot of things. We live in a very big world and an incomprehensible, massive universe that no one understands completely. It is very likely we will never understand it all. The same applies to our lives. You can't see inside others and really know what's going on with them. In fact, there are times when we don't even know what's going on inside ourselves. We can't know everything science knows. And even in science, knowledge evolves. That's the way life is. Things change. Technology changes everything, and fast. Culture and societal expectations change. People change. People tend to change when they go through different stages of life. Change is inevitable. The only realistic option is probably to just adjust to change by following the two rules: Do no harm, and do the best you can with the resources available to you. It's also a good idea to learn from your mistakes.

Most of us have gone down the wrong path at one time or another and then learned a lesson or two from the experience. Sometimes we need to take a job before we know it's not what we really want. And the opposite can happen, too. Some of us take a job only to fulfill our needs during a brief time, but we then discover the job opens a career path we never expected that fits us perfectly. Sometimes we can get enmeshed in a relationship that seemed promising in the beginning, but then... well, you know. There are many people who get on a path that leads them to unhappiness, and for a number of reasons they get trapped there. They stay on that same path and try to fight it. Here are a few lessons about your path in life. The path you are on doesn't care about your intentions. Fighting it is pointless; you can't make it conform to you. You can either conform to it, unhappily resist, or move to another path. Of course, along the way there is blame and you can feel like a victim. Here is the big question in this discussion. How do you get unstuck?

First, there is nothing wrong with changing paths, changing goals, or reassessing everything. You have power in this, but if you cede your power to others or an organization, you have betrayed yourself. As we wrote in *Freedom To Change*, if you identify as a victim, you must learn how to stop it. You have to realize you are a survivor. You are here, and you have some power and control. If you are in a bad relationship or in a bad path, change directions, backtrack, or move to another path. Make changes.

The big secret here is really one of control. You can't know everything with certainty, nor can you even know most things with certainty. As we have already said, our beliefs, feelings, and emotions can mislead us. So, what's left? That's easy. The one thing you control in life right now is *what you do*. If you are able to, raise your right arm in the air or wiggle your feet. Look around. Say something out loud. You can choose to read. You choose where your time goes. You have the power to do at least one, if not all, of the things we just mentioned. There are many other things we could ask you to do, but you get it. You control your actions. You are either a master of your life, **OR** you cede control to your unconscious and/or to others.

a. To complete this exercise, you will make another drawing. Here is a hint about it. The more detailed you make this drawing, the more you'll get from it. In the space below, draw yourself on the path you are on... first, think about how you'll depict a path in life. Think about how and where you'll draw yourself on the path. There will be other people, objects, barriers, and obstacles if they exist, etc. in the drawing. Finally, if it's possible, show where the path leads.

Daily Journal

_____

_____

_____

_____

_____

_____

_____

_____

_____

_____

_____

_____

_____

EXERCISE 23: STRIVING FOR SUPERIORITY

In *Freedom To Change*, we presented a rather long discussion about the concept known as "Striving For Superiority." Here we'll only provide a simple definition of it. For us, it starts with an assumption. We assume that the vast majority of people want to lead a meaningful life and be something better or greater than they are at any given time. Essentially, we are striving to be something superior to what we are at the present moment. We are continually striving for more, to become better and greater. It's a simple concept that can be easy to embrace. We also understand that there are some people who just want things to stay the same, to not lose what they already have, or to maybe just enjoy their retirement years. If you are raising a family, in school, or have a job, chances are that somewhere lurking in your thoughts is the desire to become a bit better, to have more, to learn more, to master some task or topic—to be superior to what you are now. So what we would like you to ask yourself at this point is what is it—*exactly*—that guides your decisions and behavior on this path to superiority?

At the beginning of this workbook we mentioned the idea of self-coaching and having a mentor. The mentor was your higher or true self—the person you are aspiring to be. When faced with choices and decisions, we asked you to act in accordance with what the person you are trying to be would do. In a way, it's like asking yourself, "What would a better or enhanced version of me do?" Of course, in order to make this work, you have to then act in accordance with what you determine your "higher" or "true self" would do. This is where our habits and beliefs can cause problems. Remember that we are creatures of habit, that we make a lot of unconscious decisions, and that we often take the path of least resistance without giving much thought to the alternatives.

a. Go back a couple pages and take a good look at the things you drew in Exercise 22. Pay close attention to how you drew yourself and the details of your drawing. Now, answer the following questions.

1. What is the expression on your face?

_____

2. How large is the drawing of you in comparison to the other people and things?

_____

3. Did you draw hands on yourself?

_____

4. If so, are they controlling anything?

_____

5. If there are no hands, could it mean that you are in a situation that you believe isn't under your control?

_____

6. Is the path you drew a rut, or does it have walls or barriers?

_____

7. How many other people are in your drawing?

_____

8. Are the people helpful or are they barriers?

_____

9. Now imagine that the person you are striving to be (the mentor) existed—this is your higher self or true self. What advice would that person give you about that path?

_____

_____

_____

_____

10. What would that mentor say about the destination you were moving toward?

_____

_____

_____

_____

11. Imagine that you reached your path's destination. What would you do then?

_____

_____

_____

_____

_____

_____

Daily Journal

_____

_____

_____

_____

_____

_____

_____

_____

_____

_____

_____

_____

EXERCISE 24:
ABCD

Freedom To Change presented a variation of Albert Ellis' belief evaluation method we refer to as ABCD in decision-making. It is a simple, 4-step process. It starts by quickly **A**ssessing a situation and challenging the **B**eliefs associated with it. Then making a **C**hoice and **D**oing it. Several examples were presented including decisions that required a lot of thought and other decisions that had to be made quickly. When you **A**ssess a situation, you are essentially listing all the beliefs you have about it. You then challenge each **B**elief. That is, you determine the validity of the belief and try to find exceptions to it. When you do this, a clear **C**hoice usually emerges quickly, and then you have to **D**o what you have chosen.

Let's look at this process in an unusual way. When we asked you to create your own mentor and act in accordance with what that mentor would do, we were asking you to play a role. Let's say that someone is exceedingly rude to you and you would usually reply with some sort of sarcastic comment. But your mentor—your higher self—asks you to be a more gentle and kind person. Your mentor whispers to you to just be kind and not counterattack that person. We can tell you one reason why that might be the case. Deep down you are aware that no one can totally and fully understand what it's like to be another person. Your mentor knows that. Your mentor also knows that all you really control is what you do—and only you control the type of person you are. Your mentor is striving for superiority. By assessing and challenging your beliefs, you are engaging your higher self and giving it some input in your decisions. If that doesn't occur, what is left are your habitual responses, and then the beliefs and feelings that get stimulated take over. Here is another little secret. We always play roles in life. We sometimes play the wrong roles, and we can play a role for so long that we forget who we really are. We simply become the accumulation of our beliefs, the feelings associated with them, and whatever our habits are. It's important to keep in mind that a lot of our personality traits are habits that have become so ingrained that, in some situations, we never realize that we have choices. One of the main assertions in *Freedom To Change* is that we are creations, not compilations. We have the ability to recreate ourselves, if we choose to do so.

a. Let's begin by thinking about how much your beliefs and habits control you. On a scale of 0% to 100%, how much influence do you think your beliefs and habits have over you?

_____

b. Now raise your right hand and put it down, or speak a sentence aloud. Look to the left with your eyes. Look to the right. On a scale of 0% to 100%, how much influence did your beliefs and habits have on those behaviors?

_____

c. Finally, think about that higher self—your mentor. Ask that higher self how much control you have over your life right now. Of course, you may have some health or money issues, but in either case you have *some* control. How you react to it is under your control, right? Chances are that you do have some control in your life. So, on a scale of 0% to 100%, what percentage of your life would your mentor say is under your control?

_____

_____

Daily Journal

_____

_____

_____

_____

_____

_____

_____

_____

_____

_____

_____

EXERCISE 25:
BEFORE YOU DEPART

In essence, we are moving toward an imaginary future in life; that's what the concept of striving for superiority is all about. It is usually a future with some happiness, contentment, success, and a sense of accomplishment. Even if you just want to "live a normal life," that implies some sort of happiness or contentment.

a. Define what happiness means to you:

_____

_____

b. What are the things you need to be happy?

_____

_____

_____

c. Define what contentment means to you:

_____

_____

d. Define what success means to you:

_____

_____

e. What do you have to have, or do, to be a success in life?

_____

_____

_____

f.   What are the things you want to accomplish in life?

_____

_____

_____

_____

g.   Life ends, and as far as we know, no one gets out alive. Chances are that when you depart this life, you'll be missed by someone. What are the things that your mentor (your higher self) *would want other people to say*—and believe—about you when you depart this life?

_____

_____

_____

_____

_____

Daily Journal

EXERCISE 26:
BACK TO ABCD

We want to remind you that as you have been working on this workbook, there are three goals you are also supposed to be working on. Bring to mind the one goal that is the most important to you right now. In addition, bring to mind one key sticking point or issue hindering your ability to fulfill that goal. For example, let's say the goal is to get a better job for all the obvious reasons. The sticking point might be that you need to get some sort of training or certification to get the job you want, and that takes time and a lot of effort.

a. What is your most important goal that came to mind?

_____

_____

b. Let's **A**ssess it by listing all the major beliefs you have about it. Examples could be that you believe a particular person is impeding you, that you don't have the time or energy, why you believe you want it, what you believe you will get if you achieve it, etc. There are probably at least five or more related beliefs.

_____

_____

_____

_____

_____

_____

_____

c. Now, take a look at all of the beliefs you listed above and challenge the **B**eliefs. Look for an exception to every one of them. The term *exception* means you are trying to show why the belief is not *completely* true or valid. Keep in mind that all beliefs have exceptions. Odds are that even the goal itself—meaning what you hope to get from accomplishing it—has exceptions. A real example is this: An individual wanted to obtain a doctoral degree because the person believed it would bestow high status and lead to making a lot of money and a prestigious job. Here is the simple way to challenge those beliefs. The doctoral degree won't, in and of itself, do any of those things. All of the things the person wants from the degree fully depend on the person—what he or she does. So look at your beliefs about your goal and challenge them.

_____

_____

_____

_____

_____

_____

_____

d. Chances are that after you challenged the beliefs, some very clear choices emerged. At least one choice became obvious. Note that we aren't saying to give up on the goal. All we are doing here is clarifying your choices about what you need to do. Can you **C**hoose a good course of action? Which course of action is it?

_____

_____

_____

e. Can you **D**o what you chose? When will you do it?

_____

_____

Daily Journal

_____

_____

_____

_____

_____

_____

_____

_____

_____

_____

_____

_____

_____

EXERCISE 27:
USING ABCD ON YOUR MENTOR

The idea of using the person you are striving to be as your mentor is probably something you were introduced to in this workbook. Maybe not, but we want to do something unique with that idea. Start by thinking about who that person is. Who is that higher self or true self you are aspiring to be? What does that person want you to do? What does that person want you to spend your time doing? How does that person want you to deal with your relationships? How does that person want you to deal with your responsibilities? What does that person want you to achieve in the future?

Once you consider those questions, form your answers into beliefs about your higher self. You can start this process by answering the questions below. Sometimes it is best to just write the first thing that comes to mind.

a. I believe my higher self is:

_____

_____

b. I believe my higher self wants:

_____

_____

c. I believe my higher self wants my most important relationship to be:

_____

_____

d. I believe my higher self wants my work to be:

_____

_____

e. As far as my health is concerned, I believe my higher self:

_____

_____

f. As far as my problems are concerned, I believe my higher self:

_____

_____

g. As far as my strengths are concerned, I believe my higher self:

_____

_____

h. With respect to my greatest accomplishments, I believe my higher self:

_____

_____

i. With respect to my friends, I believe my higher self:

_____

_____

j. My higher self wants me to spend more time on:

_____

_____

k. Assuming you have completed the list above, let's do the unusual. In the extra space under each belief you listed, challenge it. Try to think of an exception or anything else that might indicate that it is false.

l. Now, do you see a clear choice?

_____

_____

Daily Journal

_____

_____

_____

_____

_____

_____

_____

_____

_____

_____

_____

_____

_____

_____

_____

_____

_____

_____

EXERCISE 28: MINDFULNESS

In *Freedom To Change*, we discussed mindfulness several times. The concept of mindfulness has evolved out of long-standing traditions in several spiritual disciplines as well as in psychology. In essence, mindfulness is performing a deliberate act that focuses your attention on the present moment. It means you experience the here-and-now without thinking about the past or future. You simply become aware of the moment. Sometimes you focus on your breathing, feelings, bodily sensations, or physical objects in your environment. It is a way to let go of future fears, past regrets, and the sense of urgency that modern life seems to bestow on us. A simple example is looking at a flower and trying to see all of its essence and facets. You might touch it to engage your tactile sense. You might smell it. You might examine its color and texture. The idea is to really focus on the task and just experience it in the moment. This can be difficult if you have never tried this before, but it is well worth the effort.

Besides being a good practice to help settle the mind and relieve anxiety, mindfulness techniques can provide many other benefits. These techniques are now a standard in what is called "positive psychology" because rather than delving into the past or assessing future possibilities, you are creating a positive and beneficial experience in the present moment. Research shows that engaging in mindfulness reduces stress and is a good relaxation method. It can help with depression and anxiety. Mindfulness can assist in recovery from illness and can also help with some physical ailments such as high blood pressure.

Aside from focusing your attention on an object to achieve mindfulness, perhaps the easiest method is what is referred to as focused breathing. It's simple. Read the brief instructions below and then try it.

a. Focused Breathing: Close your eyes and start a slow and silent count to yourself as you breathe. Breathe in, hold it for a moment, and then breathe out while thinking "one" to yourself. Repeat it and think "two," and so on. It helps to really try to sense the air moving through your lips and nose. Try to do it to at least a count of 30. The first time you do this, you might find your mind wandering, so when you catch your attention waning, refocus on the counting and the sensation of the air while you breathe in and out. Go ahead and try it.

Did it work? _____

How do you feel? _____

_____

b. Body Scan: Lie down or sit comfortably. Close your eyes and for a moment or two, focus on your breathing. Then try to focus on the sensations you experience in various body parts. Start with one leg and focus only on what that leg feels like. Take a few moments to really sense the leg. Then move to the other leg. Then move to your arms, one at a time, and do the same. Then focus on your shoulders. Then your face. Go ahead and try it.

Did it work? _____

How do you feel? _____

_____

c. Walk About: This is often called a walking mindfulness method, although that doesn't really capture the essence of it. Here is what you should try. You should take a brief walk through the room you are in right now. Go slowly and examine everything. If there are pictures, look at them. Look at each of the objects in the room, and give them your full attention. Don't let thoughts about cleaning up or arranging things distract you. If such a thought enters your mind, you need to acknowledge it and then let it go, moving on to the next object.

Did it work? _____

How do you feel? _____

_____

Mindfulness takes practice, but it is a good way to calm your mind and thoughts. We ask you to start practicing one of these methods on a routine basis. In the other workbooks in this series, there are several more techniques that will be recommended. But for now, it's a good thing to find something simple you can easily do.

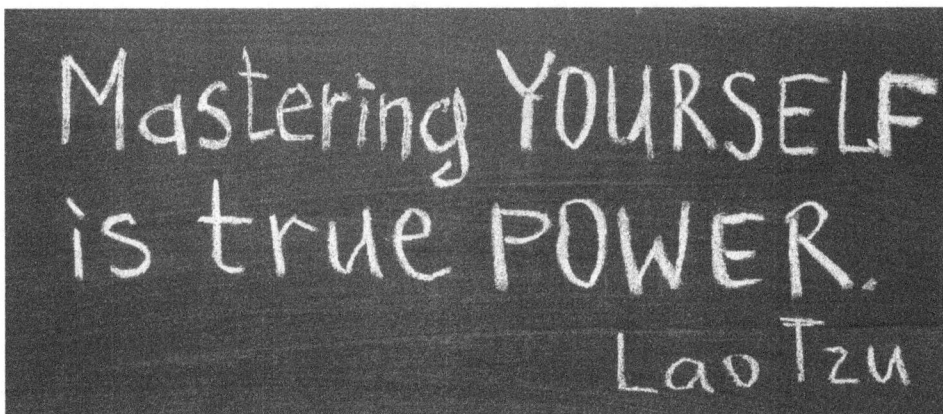

Mastering YOURSELF is true POWER. Lao Tzu

Daily Journal

_____

_____

_____

_____

_____

_____

_____

_____

_____

_____

_____

_____

_____

_____

EXERCISE 29:
THE PATH

One of the main purposes of this workbook has been to provide a systematic way for you to see your True Path and at least get a glimpse of what we call your True Self or Higher Self. We want to impress upon you that your meaning in life is something you create. You control what you do, and what you do creates who and what you are, or at least it creates the "way you are." Maybe there is some higher purpose that has been bestowed upon you through your human nature or by some higher power. That's up to you to determine. Countless philosophers, spiritual leaders, and many others have expressed a deep thought about our purpose here. They say your purpose in this life is to become the best you can be, taking into account all of your personal characteristics and abilities. In essence, it means living your life in ways that express what and who you truly are. You make those choices. What that means is that *you* create your path in life. Sure, there are lots of seemingly random events and people who pop up in life, but each of us chooses what we'll do with those encounters. We can change our current path, or leave it and move on to another. It's up to each of us.

Before we move on, we want you to answer a simple question. You don't have to write it out; just answer it to yourself. How are you doing on the three goals you set for yourself? Whether you are succeeding or not, what we want to do here, in our next-to-last exercise, is take a look at the current path you are on. We want you to look way, way down that path and see where it goes.

a. Let's imagine you fulfill your needs and your goals on the path you are on. Do you have to set more goals?

_____

_____

b. What is your underlying goal for being on your present path?

_____

_____

c. What are you seeking on your path?

_____

_____

d. Does your path allow you to be the best you can be?

_____

e. Does your path allow you to express who and what you truly are?

_____

f. Since we assume that all of us create our path through our choices, what purpose in your life have you created so far?

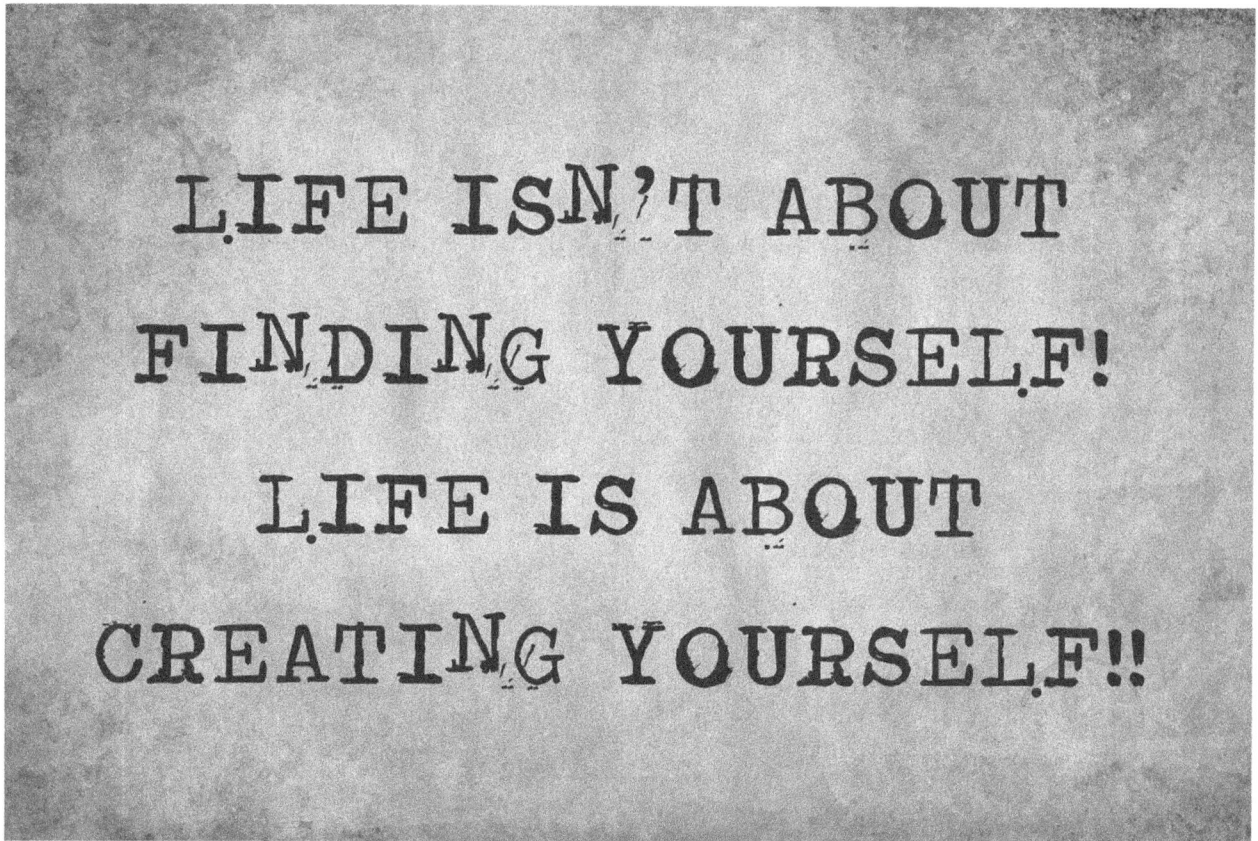

_____

_____

_____

_____

_____

LIFE ISN'T ABOUT
FINDING YOURSELF!
LIFE IS ABOUT
CREATING YOURSELF!!

Daily Journal

_____

_____

_____

_____

_____

_____

_____

_____

_____

_____

_____

_____

EXERCISE 30:
MOVING ON

In Exercise 22 we posed a question that is rooted in science. We asked if a top weighs the same when it is stationary as it does when it is spinning. The answer is "no," the top does not weigh the same in both conditions. The spinning top weighs more. We won't say why. If you are interested in it, you can do a bit of research. Our point is that beliefs don't matter. What matters is what we do. Beliefs and feelings can control us, but only if we allow them to do so. In the workbooks that follow, we go much deeper into the relationship between beliefs and feelings. But that's all optional and up to you to decide to do. What we do want to say, however, is that feelings and beliefs can be made irrelevant. You can't make them go away, but you can challenge them and make them irrelevant. Think of it this way. There are some things you dreaded or simply didn't like doing. Chances are, the first time you went to the dentist or got a shot, you had some feelings and emotions emerge. Maybe they still do. But it is just as likely that you have learned to ignore your feelings and do some things that, in the long run, are both healthy and good decisions. To end this workbook, we ask that you to try to set aside your feelings and beliefs, and consider the following questions:

a. Who and what do you want to be? How would you describe the ideal you?

_____

_____

_____

_____

b. How do you want to lead your life? What are the things you want to consistently and routinely do?

_____

_____

_____

_____

c. How do you want your relationships to be? Who are the people you want to spend your time and life with?

_____

_____

_____

_____

d. What do you want to spend your time doing?

_____

_____

_____

_____

e. Finally, when you are old and less vibrant than you are now, what are the things you want to do?

_____

_____

_____

_____

Daily Journal

www.ingramcontent.com/pod-product-compliance
Lightning Source LLC
Chambersburg PA
CBHW080053280326
41934CB00014B/3304

* 9 7 8 0 9 6 5 5 3 9 2 3 4 *